LISTENING FOR GOD

THROUGH

ACTS

Lectio Divina Bible Studies

wesleyan
publishing
house

Indianapolis, Indiana

Beacon Hill Press of Kansas City
Kansas City, Missouri

Copyright © 2006 by The Wesleyan Church
Published by Wesleyan Publishing House
Indianapolis, Indiana 46250
Printed in the United States of America

ISBN-13: 978-0-89827-333-5
ISBN-10: 0-89827-333-1

Written by Mark Moore

ABOUT THE
LECTIO DIVINA
BIBLE STUDIES

ectio divina, Latin for *divine reading,* is the ancient Christian practice of communicating with God through the reading and study of Scripture. Throughout history, great Christian leaders including John Wesley have used and adapted this ancient method of interpreting Scripture. This Bible study builds on this practice, introducing modern readers of the Bible to the time-honored tradition of "listening for God" through His Word. In this series, the traditional *lectio divina* model has been revised and expanded for use in group Bible study. Each session in this study includes the following elements. (Latin equivalents are noted in italics.)

- Summary   A brief overview of the session.
  Epitome

- Silence   A time of quieting oneself prior to
  Silencio   reading the Word.

- Preparation   Focusing the mind on the central
  Praeparatio   theme of the text.

- Reading   Carefully reading a passage of
  Lectio   Scripture.

- Meditation   Exploring the meaning of the Bible
  Meditatio   passage.

- Contemplation   Yielding oneself to God's will.
  Contemplatio

- Prayer   Expressing praise, thanksgiving,
  Oratio   confession, or agreement to God.

- Incarnation   Resolving to act on the message of
  Incarnatio   Scripture.

The Lectio Divina Bible Studies invite readers to slow down, read Scripture, meditate upon it, and prayerfully respond to God's Word.

CONTENTS

INTRODUCTION

The Acts of the Apostles reads as a sequel, second after the Gospel of Luke. Most likely penned by the same author, Acts is equally orderly, well-researched, and clearly written. It reports the birth, infancy, and explosive growth of the Church of Jesus Christ, picking up the story at the day of Jesus' ascension and continuing to approximately A.D. 63.

Acts centers around the same protagonist as does Luke's Gospel, Jesus of Nazareth. In this second book, however, Jesus speaks on only two occasions—in chapter 1, witnessed by a crowd of people; and again in chapter 9, seen and heard clearly by only one man. Nevertheless, Jesus' presence pervades the book from beginning to end.

As in any good sequel, the supporting characters in Acts grow and mature, and new characters are added as the story unfolds.

Chief among the new characters is the Holy Spirit, who enters energetically in chapter 2.

The dramatic action in Acts is every bit as heart-pounding as in the Gospel: the conversion of three thousand people in one day, the stoning of Stephen, the imprisonment of faithful followers, the transformation of venomous Saul into fearless Paul.

Acts ends suddenly, leaving the action unresolved. What will become of the fledgling church? Christians have been writing the longer ending to this book over two millennia. The open ending also leaves room for a third in the trilogy, yet to be written—it will pick up on the fulfillment day of the promise spoken by two angels: "'Men of Galilee,' they said, 'why do you stand here looking into the sky? This same Jesus, who has been taken from you into heaven, will come back in the same way you have seen him go into heaven'" (1:11).

THE ASCENDING SAVIOR

Listening for God through Acts 1:1–14

SUMMARY

T he stunned disciples peered up into the thickening clouds, speechless, until startled by the presence of angels. Jesus had risen from the dead. He was really there, walking with them, discussing the kingdom of God with them, breaking bread with them; then in a moment, He was gone.

The men dressed in white reassured the disciples that Jesus would return again; but this was not what they expected the Messiah to do. He had already returned from the grave, and now He was supposed to reunite Israel and establish His mighty kingdom.

Jesus did begin building God's kingdom that day; He just didn't do it in the way anyone on earth expected. His simple promise of the Holy Spirit foreshadowed the coming power that would enable the disciples, ordinary fisherman, to lead a revolution that has changed the world.

As you meditate on this passage, put yourself in the disciples' shoes, experiencing the myriad of emotions they must have felt as their Savior ascended.

SILENCE ✝ LISTEN FOR GOD

Begin by taking a few deep breaths, allowing your pulse to slow. Ask God to take away any distractions. Listen for His soft voice. Hear His promises. Hear His commissions.

PREPARATION ✝ FOCUS YOUR THOUGHTS

Have you ever had a close friend or family member move away? Have you ever watched the plane carrying the person you love disappear into a fog of clouds?

Experience those feelings again.

READING ✝ HEAR THE WORD

Although we don't know for certain the authorship of the book of Acts, a few clues lean largely in the direction of Luke, the physician and Gospel writer. Theophilus, the recipient of this book, was also the recipient of the Gospel of Luke, where he was addressed as "most excellent," possibly referring to a high governmental position. The author addressing Theophilus in the introduction claims to have written a previous book chronicling the life of Jesus. Luke was one of a few of Paul's close travel companions and proves to be the most logical author of Acts.

The disciples were surprised by Jesus' ascension in this passage because traditional Jewish messiology held that the Anointed One would come and restore the nation of Israel to a place of prominence and power as God's chosen people. This wasn't the first plot twist Jesus offered in the story of the Messiah. His suffering and death were not humanly expected parts of the restoration process, especially not His execution as a criminal.

But the Ascension, like the Crucifixion, was a vital part in God's plan for restoration. In the Gospel of John Jesus encourages His disciples, telling them that though He must go back to the One Who sent Him, He was sending another, a Comforter, who would flood them with grace and power. The promised gift from the Father exploded onto the scene shortly after Jesus left, and the church ignited.

Read Acts 1:1–14 slowly with a spirit of prayer, asking God to open your eyes to the meaning of the text.

MEDITATION ✝ ENGAGE THE WORD

Meditate on Acts 1:1–5

The writer of the book of Acts addressed his familiar friend, Theophilus, with a reminder of his last writings which covered "all that Jesus began to do and to teach" (1:1). Imagine being a news reporter for your local paper and your job assignment is to chronicle the life of the most famous man who ever lived: Jesus of Nazareth. What would you write about? What stories would you highlight?

Recall the Gospel accounts of the life and ministry of Jesus. What was the main point of Jesus' life? What was the heart of His message?

In verse 5 Jesus contrasts the baptism with water that John facilitated with the coming baptism of the Holy Spirit by fire. What is the difference between these two baptisms?

Meditate on Acts 1:6–8

The disciples were constantly missing the point. They made assumptions about how God was going to act, how Israel would be restored. Can you think of an area in your life in which you may be missing the point with God? Do you have a certain way you think He should act? How do you react when He doesn't meet your expectations?

Jesus didn't answer the disciples' questions with specifics. He did make them a promise: they would receive the Holy Spirit and be witnesses of His love to the entire world. What are some promises God has made to you that haven't necessarily clarified your questions but moved you beyond them? What are some things you expect from God based on your own perceptions and what are some things about God can you be sure of?

Read the sidebar quote from David Kirk. What does he mean by the "final kingdom of shalom"? List a few of the many ways we are to be signs of the kingdom of God.

> We are living "between the times" — the time of Christ's resurrection and the new age of the Spirit, and the time of fulfillment in Christ. Life in the Spirit is a pledge, a "down-payment," on the final kingdom of shalom. In the meantime, we are to be signs of the kingdom which is, and which is coming.
>
> —David Kirk

Meditate on Acts 1:9–11

The scene of Jesus disappearing seems to come right out of Hollywood. What is the significance of His ascension through the clouds?

The angels reassured the awestruck disciples that Jesus would return in a similar manner. What do you think that means? Is He literally going to come back riding the clouds? How do you picture His second coming happening?

Read the sidebar quote from William Temple. How do you understand the accessibility of Jesus after His ascension compared to the days of His ministry? Is there ever a time when you are not in the presence of God?

> In the days of His earthly ministry, only those could speak to him who came where He was: if He was in Galilee, men could not find Him in Jerusalem; if He was in Jerusalem, men could not find Him in Galilee. His Ascension means that He is perfectly united with God; we are with Him wherever we are present to God; and that is everywhere and always.
>
> — William Temple

Meditate on Acts 1:12–14

Examine closely the scenario of the disciples and the women joining together in incessant prayer. What characteristics of true Christian community can you draw from this picture?

Considering His mother and brothers' previous confusion concerning Jesus' ministry, how do you think their perception of Jesus changed after being witnesses to His death, resurrection, and ascension?

As you meditate on this passage, envision sitting in the Upper Room with this group. Feel the tension of sorrow and joy, the confusion of a missing Messiah, the excitement of what's to come.

CONTEMPLATION ✝ REFLECT AND YIELD

Do you find it hard to follow God when you are confused by His actions? Does God always meet your expectations?

Read the sidebar quote from Anatole France. In His sovereignty, God often works without being noticed or praised. What circumstances in your life, which

> Chance is perhaps the pseudonym of God when he does not wish to sign his work.
> —Anatole France

you previously attributed to *chance,* may have been the anonymous workings of God?

Oratio PRAYER ✝ RESPOND TO GOD

After the awesome experience of Jesus ascending into heaven, the disciples, along with the women followers, gathered in an upper room and *prayed constantly*. What would it look like for you to pray constantly?

Pray that God will give you a spirit of continuous prayer.

INCARNATION ✦ LIVE THE WORD

Take the assignment of being a news reporter seriously; but instead of writing Jesus' life events, journal the top stories of God's amazing work and love in your life. Record times of rescue, forgiveness, and faithfulness. Share these events with a friend from your group.

THE SPARK THAT IGNITED A CHURCH

Listening for God through Acts 2:32–47

SUMMARY

The Messiah had come. Jesus' ministry had fulfilled the promises of the prophets of old, and now His promise of the advent of a great Comforter was fulfilled as Peter addressed the crowd and sparked a flame that ignited a worldwide movement of followers of Christ—the church.

The truth of God's Word—the reality of His holiness, the imminence of His justice, and the efficacy of His grace—sliced open the hearts of His chosen people. God himself had paid the debt for the sin of His children. Peter's call to repentance and cleansing was received by three thousand penitent hearts that day of Pentecost.

The presence of the Holy Spirit unified this large group nearly instantaneously, establishing the Church as one body with many parts dedicated to the service of one mission. The early Church remains for us a lasting example of sacrificial love and selfless devotion.

SILENCE ✝ LISTEN FOR GOD

Quiet your heart before the Lord. Think of one attribute of God (for example, faithfulness, holiness, righteousness). Repeat the word slowly, softly.

PREPARATION ✝ FOCUS YOUR THOUGHTS

Have you ever been present at the birth of a child? Have you ever been a witness to the beginning of life? Imagine experiencing the same sense of creation as an early Christian at the birth of the universal Church.

READING ✝ HEAR THE WORD

In the fourteenth chapter of John's Gospel, Jesus comforted His disciples as He explained to them the motive behind His coming suffering and death. As He broke bread with them in the Upper Room, Jesus made a promise that the Father would send a helper, a *parakleôtos*. Jesus insisted that He had to leave them in order for the Spirit to come. Jesus wasn't the only one who foretold the outpouring of the Holy Spirit. God made this promise to His people through the prophets, a fact Peter referred to by quoting the prophet Joel in his Pentecost message.

Peter also used the book of Psalms in his apology for the kingship of Jesus. The quote from David comes from Psalm 110 and is an example of prophetic poetry looking ahead at the relationship between Jesus and His Father. Peter pointed out that David was not speaking of himself in this psalm, a point that opened the eyes of many listening to him.

In the portion of Psalm 110 not referenced by Peter, David went on to call this "lord" [Jesus] a priest in the order of Melchizedek, directing his Jewish audience back to Abraham and ultimately the initial promise of salvation.

Read Acts 2:32–47 aloud twice, paying special attention to verses 42–47.

MEDITATION ✝ ENGAGE THE WORD

Meditate on Acts 2:32–36

These four simple verses address one of the most complex concepts in all of Scripture: the inner working of the Trinity. The Father raised the Son to His right hand. The Holy Spirit was promised and sent by both the Father and the Son. They are all three distinct persons yet one God and Lord. How do you understand the Trinity? What does this passage say about the different roles of each member of this holy triad?

Peter quoted David in his Pentecost sermon. What was David's understanding of the Messiah? Do you think Jesus would have fit David's messianic mold? Read Psalm 110 as you meditate on this question.

Read the sidebar quote from John Wesley. What do you think Wesley meant when he spoke of setting up the kingdom of heaven on earth? You don't have to be a pastor to be one of Wesley's hundred. What is stopping you from joining this group?

> Give me one hundred preachers who fear nothing but sin and desire nothing but God, and I care not whether they be clergymen or laymen, they alone will shake the gates of Hell and set up the kingdom of Heaven upon Earth.
>
> —John Wesley

Meditate on Acts 2:37–41

Do you remember a time when God pierced your false defenses and opened your heart to His life? Have you ever seen this

THE SPARK THAT IGNITED A CHURCH 23

happen in someone else's life? What is the true cause of this brokenness?

> The Spirit-filled life is not a special, deluxe edition of Christianity. It is part and parcel of the total plan of God for his people.
> —A. W. Tozer

Read the sidebar quote from A. W. Tozer. Peter's call for repentance and baptism came with a gift, the Holy Spirit. Have you ever thought that being Spirit-filled was something for super-Christians? What does it mean to be full of the Spirit?

The outpouring of the Holy Spirit occurred after Jesus' resurrection and ascension and after the disciples believed Jesus as the Christ. Is there a time lapse between the moment of belief and the gift of the Holy Spirit for Christians today?

Read the sidebar quote from Charles Spurgeon. Peter definitely served it up hot. Has the fire of your baptism seemed more like a waning flame lately? What are some ways to keep your relationship with God aflame?

> Religion is a dish to be served hot; once it becomes lukewarm it is sickening. Our baptism must be with the Holy Ghost and with fire if we would win the masses to hear the gospel.
> —Charles Spurgeon

Meditate on Acts 2:42–47

This is the premier passage of biblical community. Does the picture described here exemplify your church? How might these verses be transposed in modern culture?

The believers sold their possessions and held everything in common in an act that many call *Christian socialism*. What were the benefits of this economic venture? Is it possible to accomplish this in today's market? Should we attempt to move back to this sort of communal economy?

> The people of God are not merely to mark time, waiting for God to step in and set right all that is wrong. Rather, they are to model the new heaven and new earth, and by so doing awaken longing for what God will someday bring to pass.
>
> —Philip Yancey

Read the sidebar quote from Philip Yancey. Now that Jesus is in heaven and the Spirit has come, what is the Church supposed to do? In what ways can we model the kingdom of heaven on earth?

Look past the socio-economic message of this description of the early Church. What does it say about the correct spirit of the Church? Does anything in your church need to change for true fellowship to occur? How can you be part of that change?

CONTEMPLATION ✝ REFLECT AND YIELD

Verses 42-47 show the *agape* love of early believers. Do you think the same type of unity is occurring among Christians today? Why or why not?

What is the current Church devoted to?

PRAYER ✝ RESPOND TO GOD

Throughout Acts we see believers praying together fervently before the Lord. Pray together that God will pour out His Spirit on your group, your church, your community.

INCARNATION ✝ LIVE THE WORD

Sharing a meal together is a critical part of fellowship. Families strengthen around the dinner table; friends grow closer when they eat together. Plan a meal with either family or friends this week. Have everyone bring something to share. Also invite someone who you know needs to feel a sense of community.

THE WISDOM OF
A PHARISEE

Listening for God through Acts 5:27–42

SUMMARY

Founded on the belief that salvation is rendered by the death and resurrection of Jesus Christ, the movement known as the Way began to spread. Fearful Jewish leaders sought to squelch any momentum of this rising faction by having its main proponents brought before their high court. Peter and the other apostles stood on trial for preaching the name of Jesus. These Jewish officials were enraged that they were being blamed for executing the Messiah to the point that they wanted to put to death anyone who spoke His name.

One of their own, though, a Pharisee, brought a word of wisdom to their counsel. He advised his brothers to let God work things out. If God was truly behind this movement, then not even the death of its leaders would stop it. God would work His will regardless of the players involved. And they did not want to be on the side that warred against God. The council listened to him, and the apostles—after being scorned and beaten—were released.

Upon being released, the apostles proclaimed the good news of the salvation of Jesus Christ with even more zeal.

SILENCE ✝ LISTEN FOR GOD

Close your eyes and sit in silence for five minutes. As your mind wanders, gently draw it back to silence by whispering the prayer, "Lord Jesus, have mercy on me."

PREPARATION ✝ FOCUS YOUR THOUGHTS

Have you ever been faced with a major life decision? Was it a time when the will of God wasn't exactly clear? How did you seek out the will of the Father?

READING ✝ HEAR THE WORD

Peter and the other apostles were taken before the Sanhedrin, the highest Jewish court. This court worked primarily like our Supreme Court works today. It saw cases the lower courts could not decide on, and it interpreted and enforced the main law of the people—for them, the Law of Moses. The Sanhedrin consisted of seventy-one members and two major schools of thought: the Pharisees and the Sadducees. The deciding difference of these two parties was the belief in the resurrection of the dead, which the Pharisees held to be true and the Sadducees did not.

Gamaliel was a Pharisee, a wise and respected man. He was one of the apostle Paul's main teachers. Gamaliel's wisdom and sensitivity to the will of God may have been the first seed of openness to Jesus' resurrection planted deep within Paul's heart.

Read Acts 5:27–42 and visualize yourself sitting among the council, listening to the testimony of the apostles and Gamaliel's warning.

MEDITATION ✝ ENGAGE THE WORD

Meditate on Acts 5:27–28

Standing before the highest court in the land, Peter and the other apostles were forbidden to speak of the name of Jesus. How is the ruling of the Sanhedrin similar with recent rulings given by the Supreme Court in the United States? In what ways are we restricted from speaking the name of Jesus?

Discuss the nature of religious freedom in America.

Read the sidebar quote from G. K. Chesterton. We see glimpses of it today, but a time may be coming when even speaking the name of Jesus will require great courage. In what countries right now is it a crime to speak openly about Christianity? Would you have the courage to speak His name?

> Brave men are all vertebrates; they have their softness on the surface and their toughness in the middle.
>
> –G. K. Chesterton

Meditate on Acts 5:29–32

Peter's passionate response raises for us an interesting question: when is it permissible to go against a direct order of the state? How do we balance the principle of respecting those in authority over us against following the truth of God?

Using verses 30–32, define the gospel, the good news of Jesus Christ.

Read the sidebar quote from Daniel Webster. Do you struggle with accepting the fantastic gospel story as a reality? Could this story of Jesus be just that: a simple, moral story? To have any meaning, is it necessary for the

> My heart has always assured and reassured me that the gospel of Christ must be a Divine reality.
>
> –Daniel Webster

events explained by Peter to the Sanhedrin to be factual? Do you think the disciples would have risked their lives for a myth? Would you give up your life for a story?

Meditate on Acts 5:33–39

Gamaliel's address to the members of the council was poignant and wise; yet it came from a seemingly unlikely source. Has God ever spoken His wisdom to you through an unusual source? Considering God as the source of all truth, what are some other places one can find His truth outside the general Christian haunts?

Gamaliel attributed the Way with other revolts that had occurred in the area. Is Christianity truly a revolt against Judaism? Explain the connection between the Old Covenant and the New Covenant. How did Jesus view these two testaments?

Read the sidebar quote from C. S. Lewis. How are you affected by your circle of friends? Is your current group of friends making you wiser or dumbing you down? What are some things you can do to help improve your own wisdom?

> The next best thing to being wise oneself is to live in a circle of those who are.
> —C. S. Lewis

Meditate on Acts 5:40–42

Though the apostles were set free, they still had to endure a flogging. What is the price of freedom today? Have you ever suffered for doing what is right? Would you humbly rejoice in being counted worthy to suffer disgrace for the sake of Christ?

The disciples would not—could not!—stop preaching the name of Jesus. Do feel this strong drive to preach His Word? Besides being behind a pulpit, how can you proclaim His name in your community?

CONTEMPLATION ✝ REFLECT AND YIELD

How do you know whether something is of human origin or from God? What tests can you use to help find the truth?

Read the sidebar quote from B. A. Copass. Do you find it hard to take Jesus at His word? Why do you think so much of God's truth stands shrouded in mystery?

> God has revealed many truths which He has not explained. We will just have to be content to let Him know some things we do not, and take Him at His word.
>
> —B. A. Copass

PRAYER ✝ RESPOND TO GOD

Perceiving the will of God can take a bit of trial and error. Are you currently involved in something that causes you to question whether your motive is humanly-inspired or God-driven? Pray for discernment. Pray for wisdom and understanding.

INCARNATION ✝ LIVE THE WORD

Chart out your life the way you would like to see it unfold over the next five to ten years in various areas, including vocation, marriage, children, schooling, sports. Share your dreams with God and ask Him to lead you to His will. Then ask Him for the courage required to follow your calling.

THE STONING OF STEPHEN

Listening for God through Acts 7:39–60

SUMMARY

As the movement of the Way continued to grow, the apostles found it necessary to appoint lay workers—deacons—to oversee the work of distributing food to orphans and widows, among other service tasks. Stephen was chosen as one of seven to do this job. But as Stephen began his work and shared his faith, God called him to a higher act of service.

Stephen unabashedly preached the good news of Jesus Christ and never lowered his voice in fear, even when standing before the mighty Sanhedrin. Stephen was a common disciple, but his words that day were anything but common. They were extraordinary. They were full of passion and confidence founded on the grace and love of his Savior.

As the stones began to hit—and cloaks were strewn at the feet of Saul in praise of his zealous killings—Stephen received his glorious reward as a martyr, a hero. His death had the opposite effect from what the Sanhedrin had hoped. Instead of fear, courage spread among the believers. Instead of silence, a growing war cry could be heard.

SILENCE ✝ LISTEN FOR GOD

Sit back comfortably in your chair. Close your eyes, and take slow deep breaths. Ask God to fill you with His presence with each breath.

PREPARATION ✝ FOCUS YOUR THOUGHTS

Have you ever had to exert your energy to the point of physical exhaustion? Maybe it was on the athletic field, on the job, or on your knees scrubbing layers of scum from your shower floor.

We can't fully understand the plight of the martyr but we can at least grasp the feeling of utter exhaustion.

READING ✝ HEAR THE WORD

The newly formed body of Christ grew at such a rapid pace that the twelve disciples could not do everything that needed to be done. They couldn't do all the preaching and teaching and ministry of the Word while they were caring for the physical needs of the people. The seven who were chosen by the disciples, recorded in Acts 6, were men full of the Holy Spirit and wisdom. They would be considered *deacons* in the current church, a word that comes from the Greek word *diakoneo*, which literally means "table waiter."

This didn't mean the disciples no longer had to serve people, but the majority of their time was reserved for prayer and teaching. The deacons looked after the daily affairs of the pooled resources of the early believers much like a manager would do.

As Peter did in his speech on the day of Pentecost, Stephen passionately tried to persuade the Jewish Sanhedrin by appealing to the words of their prophets who spoke of Jesus' coming, quoting passages from Amos and Isaiah. These passages prophesied, though, to the fact that the children of Israel would harden their hearts against the message of Christ.

Read Acts 7:39–60. Read this long passage slowly, and put yourself in the place of the Jewish leaders. Is your heart hardened to the will of God?

MEDITATION ✝ ENGAGE THE WORD

Meditate on Acts 7:39–43

The children of Israel were constantly turning their backs on God and running into the arms of idols. What idols in your life keep you from running to the true God? Do you find yourself in an endless cycle of putting your trust in idols rather than God?

Stephen's speech before the Sanhedrin was one of many attempts by the early Christians to share the message of Christ with the highest Jewish officials. Why were their hearts so hardened to the message of Jesus? Have you encountered this type of bitterness toward the Christian story? How did you respond?

Read the sidebar quote from Martin Luther. Why are we so easily attracted to idolatry? Are there subtle ways that we exalt simple things of nature over God?

> We easily fall into idolatry, for we are inclined thereunto by nature, and coming to us by inheritance, it seems pleasant.
> —Martin Luther

Meditate on Acts 7:44–50

In his appeal, Stephen referred to the "tabernacle of testimony," which would have symbolized for the Jewish leaders the very presence of God. Where does God's presence reside now? How can people be so close to God and still miss Him? In what ways have you been blinded to His presence?

Explain how God dwells in the church today. How can God be present at all times in and through everything? What comfort can you take from this truth?

Does God feel distant to you? He is closer than you feel Him to be. Ask Him to open your heart to recognize His presence.

Meditate on Acts 7:51–53

The chosen people of God were in many ways the worst at perceiving His work and accepting it with joy. How were they resisting the Holy Spirit? How do we resist the Holy Spirit?

The Israelites were not the only nation known for killing messengers of tough truth. What would cause an entire nation to reject the message of just one of its citizens?

Read the sidebar quote from John Calvin. What are some typical catalysts of unbelief? Has unbelief caused you to miss any of God's blessings? How do you deal with doubt and unbelief?

> No man is excluded from calling upon God, the gate of salvation is set open unto all men: neither is there any other thing which keepeth us back from entering in, save only our own unbelief.
>
> —John Calvin

Stephen spoke of the law being "put into effect through angels." I don't think that this is a huge theological issue, but what do you think he meant by that statement? Is there any great significance that angels had a hand in instituting God's law?

Meditate on Acts 7:54–60

In a moment of the leaders' fury, Stephen entered God's glorious presence a martyr. Have you heard any contemporary stories of martyrdom? Share some these stories as a group and marvel at the courage and zeal of God's saints.

Read the sidebar quote from church father Augustine. News about suicide bombers and terrorists fulfilling their callings as martyrs for their faith fills the

> Not the punishment but the cause makes the martyr.
>
> —Augustine

airwaves these days. What makes Stephen's death different from a Muslim martyr? How does culture change one's perception of true martyrdom? For what sort of causes can someone truly be considered a martyr?

Stephen carried the spirit of Christ with him until the very end, even breathing out forgiveness for his killers as he died. How was Stephen able to remain so full of love during this traumatic event? Would his reaction have been your natural instinct?

Read the quote from Søren Kierkegaard. Why doesn't the death of a martyr kill his cause? How did the movement of Jesus Christ enlarge after Stephen's death?

> The tyrant dies and his rule is over, the martyr dies and his rule begins.
>
> —Søren Kierkegaard

While actual martyrdom in North America is low, across the world hundreds of thousands of people are being imprisoned and dying each year for their faith. Yet despite overt persecution, the international church is exploding. What can the North American church learn from our international brothers and sisters?

CONTEMPLATION ✝ REFLECT AND YIELD

How did Stephen and the many martyrs who followed him affect the course of the early church? How was this persecution helpful in spreading the gospel?

Would you be willing to endure persecution, even death, for the cause of Christ? Honestly wrestle with this question.

Oratio
PRAYER ✝ RESPOND TO GOD

Stephen saw beyond this world as he looked up into the face of Jesus. He had no fear, because he saw his Comforter. He saw his Savior and the place He had prepared for him.

Pray with the same sense of comfort. Look up into heaven and seek God's face.

Incarnatio
INCARNATION ✝ LIVE THE WORD

Locate other stories of persecution, either in the Bible or modern occurrences. Try organizations like Voice of the Martyrs or Amnesty International for current statistics. Seek ways you can help these organizations. Begin by praying each morning for the persecuted.

THE CONVERSION
OF ST. PAUL

Listening for God through Acts 9:1–16

SUMMARY

The most vicious, violent opponent of the Way was chosen by God to carry Jesus' name to the Gentiles. Surprised? The early Christians couldn't believe it either. Ananias feared to go to Saul, even when sent directly by God, because Ananias had heard about this persecutor of Christians. Why would God work in this manner?

From the beginning, God's message has been about total life-transformation. He is not so concerned with making our lives better as with making our lives completely different. Saul's zeal, originally for imprisoning and killing those who believed the good news of salvation through Jesus Christ, was sanctified and turned into passion for spreading the gospel all over the world.

If God can change the heart of the "chief of sinners," how much more can He change your heart? Your story, like Paul's, will be one of complete change—beautiful reconciliation with the God and Father of all.

SILENCE ✝ LISTEN FOR GOD

Relax in the presence of your Heavenly Father. Avoid the temptation to rush through this section; instead, slowly prepare your heart for worship by reverently praising Him for the many blessings He has given you.

PREPARATION ✝ FOCUS YOUR THOUGHTS

Have you ever been driving west around the time the sun was setting and been blinded by its bright light for a brief moment? Imagine that blindness lasting for a couple of days, a couple months, a lifetime. How do you think you would feel if you suddenly went blind?

READING ✝ HEAR THE WORD

In his letter to the Philippians, we learn a little about Paul's Jewish heritage. He was what he called a "Hebrew of Hebrews"—following the letter of the law down to every jot. He was from the tribe of Benjamin and a Pharisee. His schooling as a Pharisee, under the wise Gamaliel, actually prepared the way for him to understand the resurrection of Jesus and know how to share it with other Jews.

Damascus was one of the oldest ancient cities, mentioned as far back as the time of Abraham. It was the capitol of Syria, located about 133 miles north of Jerusalem. Saul's traveling this great distance from Jerusalem showed the immense hatred he had for followers of Jesus.

Straight street, which was the address where the blind Saul was staying, was the main street of the city, also referred to as Queens street.

Ananias was yet another wise, godly man whom God placed in the life of Paul to instruct him and guide him to the truth.

Read Acts 9:1–16 twice, alternating readers every eight verses.

MEDITATION ✝ ENGAGE THE WORD

Meditate on Acts 9:1–6

Why do you think Saul was so adamantly opposed to the follow-ers of Christ? What is the significance of the flashing light at his conversion? The road? His mission in Damascus?

Jesus spoke directly, audibly, to Saul at the moment of his salva-tion. He accused Saul of persecuting Him. Why do you think Jesus personally appeared to Saul on the road to Damascus? How was Saul persecuting Jesus?

Read the sidebar quote from Joseph Alleine. How did the deep work of conversion continue to mature in Paul's life? Explain how conversion is as much a process as it is instantaneous.

> Conversion is a deep work—a heart-work. It goes throughout the man, throughout the mind, throughout the members, throughout the entire life.
> —Joseph Alleine

Did your conversion end at the altar, or did it continue to grow, mature, and open your eyes to more of God?

Meditate on Acts 9:7–9

Paul was blinded by the light and truth of Christ. While this event truly happened, it also serves as a metaphor of redemption. What does the metaphor of Paul's blindness teach us? What do you think were the reactions of the men traveling with Paul? (Remember: they saw the light but didn't hear the voice.)

Read the sidebar quote from John Milton. Think of his poetic words as referring to spiritual blindness. What causes spiritual blindness? In what ways can this sort of blindness be self-inflicted?

> O loss of sight, of thee I most complain! Blind among enemies, O worse than chains, dungeon or beggary, or decrepit age! Light, the prime work of God, to me is extinct, and all her various objects of delight annulled, which might in part my grief have eased.
>
> —John Milton

Light is a common symbol of God. What insight does the contrast of dark to light give in the area of conversion?

Read the sidebar quote from Thomas Hardy. Here, Hardy is speaking of a different kind of blindness—illusion. In your eagerness to serve Christ, have you chased after illusions? How can

> There is a condition worse than blindness, and that is, seeing something that isn't there.
>
> —Thomas Hardy

you open your eyes to the true work of God? Saul thought he was following God. He even thought God was pleased with what he was doing by persecuting this heretical sect. But he was chasing an illusion. What illusions are present in the church today?

Meditate on Acts 9:10–16

Ananias probably couldn't have been taken more off guard by God's command to go to Saul, a ruthless enemy. Have you ever been taken off guard by one of Christ's commands? Do you have enemies to whom you are called to minister? Do you struggle to feel compassion for these enemies?

God explained to Ananias that He had chosen Saul as His messenger to the Gentiles. This must have seemed an odd choice to Ananias. Have you ever questioned God about one of His chosen servants? What is God trying to teach us by choosing imperfect people to carry out His perfect will?

Read the sidebar quote from Blaise Pascal. Conversion is not a matter of intention. Intention is rendered impotent without action. Have you put all of your good intentions into action? What is stopping you from being truly changed?

> Men often take their imagination for their heart; and they believe they are converted as soon as they think of being converted.
>
> —Blaise Pascal

Do you ever feel unworthy of being called one of Christ's servants?

CONTEMPLATION † REFLECT AND YIELD

The blindness Saul experienced was both physical and spiritual. While you may not be physically blind, how is your spiritual eyesight? Are your eyes opened wide to what the Lord is doing? Or are they blinded by your own will and desires?

PRAYER ✝ RESPOND TO GOD

Examine your life before the Lord and ask Him to reveal to you how you have been working against Him. Open your heart fully to God in prayer and allow His Spirit to purify you.

INCARNATION ✝ LIVE THE WORD

Just as God spoke to Ananias concerning Saul's need, ask Him to show you a person in your life who is walking around spiritually blind. Make an effort to spend some time this week with the person God reveals. In humility, talk naturally with the person about clear spiritual vision.

PETER'S VISION CHANGES

Listening for God through Acts 10:9–23

SUMMARY

The entire scope of Jewish culture was detailed and directed by the Law of Moses, from the Ten Commandments to strict dietary rules. What the children of Israel ate was just as much a spiritual issue as adultery or murder. Peter's vision was a huge paradigm shift for the Jewish disciples and early followers of Christ. While Jesus was the Messiah—God's Anointed One to save the Jews—His salvation was not meant for just the nation of Israel.

God revealed this to Peter by showing him a change in the law. What was once considered unclean was suddenly considered clean. God immediately sent men from Cornelius the centurion to get Peter and hear his message. Gentiles were being let in on the great secret of God that Jews had kept since the time of Abraham.

Peter naturally resisted, wanting to show God his holiness; but God had changed the rules of the game. What Peter ate was no longer a sign of his devotion to God. The motivation of his heart was what mattered now.

SILENCE ✝ LISTEN FOR GOD

Part of being in the presence of God is the realization of personal sinfulness. Confess your sins to God and accept His forgiveness.

PREPARATION ✝ FOCUS YOUR THOUGHTS

Have you had a traditional Passover—or any kosher—meal? Why do you think God gave such strict food preparation guidelines to the children of Israel? Discuss a few of the dietary laws and God's possible motives.

READING ✝ HEAR THE WORD

In this passage of Acts we find Peter praying on a rooftop, a custom he learned from the Savior. A typical Jewish house at this time would normally have a rooftop that served as another room. Peter became hungry and was awaiting a kosher meal when he received this vision. The dietary laws found in the book of Leviticus shed light on this vision.

The eleventh chapter of Leviticus details what kind of food would be considered kosher. The Jews were allowed to eat only of animals that had split hooves and chewed cud; so when Peter saw a sheet with all kinds of four-legged animals on it, plus reptiles and birds, he would have been repulsed by the thought of eating them.

Cornelius was a centurion of the Roman guard. As a Gentile he was considered unclean by the Jewish Law. God radically challenged Peter's beliefs by asking him to partake of unclean food and to eat in the house of an unclean Gentile.

Read Acts 10:9–23 and focus on any word that jumps out at you. Repeat that word to yourself as you begin to meditate on God's Word.

Meditatio

MEDITATION † ENGAGE THE WORD

Meditate on Acts 10:9–10

A familiar picture of Peter is him enraptured with the business of prayer. Is setting aside times of prayer a familiar custom for you? What is your view of prayer, especially extended times of prayer?

Read the sidebar quote from Alexis Carrel. This is a great picture of prayer. But do you really feel this way about prayer?

> Prayer, like radium, is a luminous and self-generating form of energy.
>
> —Alexis Carrel

How can we change our perceptions of this sacred act? Why do you think prayer often gets the description of being boring? If your experience is different with prayer, share this with the group.

Peter understood the true nature of prayer, because he learned the art of prayer from the Master Himself. Have you had a great example of prayer in your life?

Read the sidebar quote from Frank Laubach. The story of Peter's vision displays the dialectic nature of prayer. Peter spoke to God on the rooftop, and God spoke back. Besides visions, what are some other ways that God speaks to us? Have you ever had a vision?

> Prayer at its highest is a two-way conversation—and for me the most important part is listening to God's replies.
> —Frank Laubach

Do you find that most of your prayers are one-sided? How can you turn your prayer times into a true dialogue with God?

Meditate on Acts 10:11–16

God's request of Peter wasn't a flippant food order. God was asking Peter to break the Law of Moses, a law Peter had remained obedient to since birth. And He had good reason. What rules or laws have you religiously followed since your youth that God may be asking you to break? How do you balance tradition with new revelation from God?

Read the verse from Leviticus. This should help explain the magnitude of God's request to Peter. The dietary laws recorded by Moses and followed strictly by multiple generations of Jews were not just concerned with food, but holiness. Why would God connect holiness with food in the Old Covenant? How did the New Covenant change this?

> I am the LORD your God; consecrate yourselves and be holy, because I am holy. Do not make yourselves unclean by any creature that moves about on the ground.
>
> —Leviticus 11:44

Put yourself in Peter's place. How would you have reacted to God on that rooftop? How are you reacting to God currently as He challenges and tests your beliefs? Has God ever made things clean that you once considered impure?

Meditate on Acts 10:17–23

God didn't stop at food with Peter. He challenged his thinking again by telling him to eat with Gentiles. What group could be considered modern day-Gentiles with whom God is asking the Church to fellowship? It is easy to recoil from these questions with fear of heresy, but imagine Peter's hesitance.

It is okay to tread lightly on this topic. Many voices calling for change today are laced with false motives. What are some ways you can be sure it is God, rather than your own misguided desires, changing the rules?

Read the sidebar quote from Jonathan Swift. God was show-ing Peter something that others weren't yet ready to see. Have

> Vision is the art of seeing what is invisible to others.
> —Jonathan Swift

you ever been privy to knowledge that wasn't yet public? What did you do with that knowledge?

How do you learn the art of true spiritual vision?

CONTEMPLATION ✝ REFLECT AND YIELD

What message can the Church pull from this story today? Are there things currently labeled unclean that are really clean? Why is it hard sometimes for Christians to change their perceptions on certain issues even when God reveals His truth?

PRAYER ✝ RESPOND TO GOD

Peter received this vision from God when he was up on a rooftop praying. Pray now for God's vision, His specific message for you. Then look for other times today or this week to withdraw and pray.

INCARNATION ✝ LIVE THE WORD

Create a list of beliefs that you held about God before you were saved or even early in your relationship with Him. Track how those beliefs have changed as you have matured in Christ. Are there any beliefs you know are false but you can't seem to let go of them? Discuss these with a close friend or pastor.

A FAREWELL
TO FRIENDS

Listening for God through Acts 20:17–38

SUMMARY

From the moment of conversion on the Damascus road, Paul's ministry was explosive and fast-paced. He traveled the whole stretch of the coast of the Mediterranean Sea up into Asia Minor. He journeyed to Italy, stopping at the scattered islands along the way, preaching the good news that the Messiah had come to both Jews and Gentiles.

Paul had spent over three years in Ephesus building the church there and had sent word for the elders in Ephesus to come meet him in Miletus when this passage of Acts picks up. Paul knew hardship awaited him, but his desire to do the will of the Father overshadowed any fear. In fact, the Spirit constantly reminded Paul that suffering was his lot, but nothing could slow Paul down.

Persecution merely fueled his passion.

The emotional farewell recorded here by Luke shows how personally connected Paul was to the people he preached to. He deeply cared for them and for every soul he met.

SILENCE ✝ LISTEN FOR GOD

Allow God to assuage the distractions of your mind. He is in control and has your best interests in mind. Rest in that thought today.

PREPARATION ✝ FOCUS YOUR THOUGHTS

Saying goodbye is hard, especially when you don't know the next time you will see the person. As Christians we know that we will see each other again in heaven. How does this thought help during times of emotional goodbyes?

Does it ever feel like nothing more than wishful thinking?

READING ✝ HEAR THE WORD

Paul sent word to the elders of Ephesus from the coastal city of Miletus, which is located on the western shore of modern-day Turkey where the Mediterranean and Aegean Seas meet. Paul was waiting there for a ship to take him across the Mediterranean so that he could get to Jerusalem.

Ephesus was a city with great history. Being founded in the eleventh century B.C., it was the home to many great ancient thinkers. It was also the home of the Temple of Artemis (Diana), considered one of the wonders of the ancient world. Christianity was brought there by Jews who had heard the message of John the Baptist and the teaching of Apollos. Priscilla and Aquila were well-known leaders of the church.

Paul helped solidify the church in Ephesus and spoke out openly against the great temple, making more enemies than friends with the local merchants who made their money from the temple and the multitude of tourists it attracted each year. As Paul left, he commissioned Timothy to shepherd the church of Ephesus and lead them in the way of the Lord. Paul's farewell on the shores of Miletus was a farewell not just to parishioners, but to friends.

Read Acts 20:17–38 quietly to yourself. Don't rush.

Meditatio

MEDITATION ✝ ENGAGE THE WORD

Meditate on Acts 20:17–21

Paul was directed by God to teach His word to all people, both Jews and Greeks. And Paul fulfilled this mission, although at different times he was at odds with both groups. Because he had been a zealous Pharisee, new Christians and other Gentiles feared him. Because he was an apostle of the living Christ, Jewish leaders strained to kill him.

Read the sidebar quote from Blaise Pascal. In order for people to respond to God, they need to hear His invitation. That is where

> Human beings must be known to be loved; but Divine beings must be loved to be known.
>   —Blaise Pascal

you come in. How would you rate yourself in the area of evangelism? Many people do not share their faith because they don't want to be intrusive. What are some ways you can share your faith without being pushy?

Paul reminded the leaders from Ephesus of his life example and leadership while he was with them. What would people say about you if they lived and worked with you for an extended period of time? When it comes to sharing God's message, what's a good ratio for words compared to actions?

We have all probably experienced people who lived differently from what they taught. Paul was different. He did what he said, and he encouraged these new leaders to live with the same integrity. And he encourages us to do the same today.

Meditate on Acts 20:22–24

Recall the last time you were *compelled by the Spirit*. How did you know it was the Spirit prompting you? Paul often spoke of being led by the Spirit. What did he do that put him in the place to hear from God so often? What distracts you from sensing leadings from the Spirit?

Suffering was not a new part of Paul's life. From the moment of his conversion, Paul's calling included a steady dose of suffering for the name of Christ. Why do you think Paul had to suffer so much? What did his suffering do to his ministry?

Read the sidebar quote from Augustine. Jesus' call also included extreme suffering. Is Christ's body, the Church, experi-

God had one Son on earth without sin, but never one without suffering.

—Augustine

encing the same amount of suffering today? Now, narrow the question: Has the North American church grown complacent because of a lack of suffering? Is suffering still a part of the Church's call?

Meditate on Acts 20:25–31

How was Paul "innocent of the blood of all men"? Paul was adamant that he had preached the whole will of God. What are some ways that someone could preach only a part of the will of God?

Paul was speaking to the elders of the church in Ephesus when he called them to be "shepherds of the church of God." How are the pastor and other church leaders like shepherds? In light of the priesthood of all believers, what is the difference between the minister and his or her parishioners?

Paul spoke of false prophets infiltrating the church, even from within, upon his departure. How can we spot these wolves in sheep's clothing? What are some ways we can distinguish evolving orthodoxy from heresy?

Does your church have a graceful watchdog: someone sifting through new philosophies preserving the truth? The line between guarding the truth and holding an Inquisition is thin. How do you maintain the truth while remaining open to new ideas?

Have you had an experience with one of the *wolves* Paul was referencing? How did the distortion of truth hurt the church?

Meditate on Acts 20:32–38

Paul and his companions worked hard with their own hands to supply their needs and to set an example of the kind of hard work it takes to help the weak. Do you feel the Church has lost this sense of the hard work of caring for those in need? Disaster relief at home and abroad has allowed the Church to shine, but how are local churches doing at serving their own communities?

Read the sidebar quote from Henry Wadsworth Longfellow. Have you witnessed a life that was devoted to charity and gracious acts of service? Share the stories of these great examples of love with your group.

> The life of a man consists not in seeing visions and in dreaming dreams, but in active charity and in willing service.
> —Henry Wadsworth Longfellow

Paul quoted Jesus as saying, "It is more blessed to give than to receive" (v. 35). Take a moment to meditate on that phrase. Repeat the phrase softly. Do you struggle with giving versus receiving?

This passage ends with a moving scene of the elders of the church weeping and kissing Paul. Recreate this scene in your mind. Replace your picture of Paul with your own pastor or mentor. What does this scene look like in your context?

CONTEMPLATION ✝ REFLECT AND YIELD

Paul was certain of only this concerning his upcoming trip to Jerusalem: prison and hardship awaited him. Yet he did not hesitate to go. How would you react if God called you into imminent suffering? Would you go with courage and faith?

PRAYER ✝ RESPOND TO GOD

Ministers of the whole truth of God often walk through this life isolated. Pray for your pastor and other leaders of your church. Pray that they will always be faithful to the call God has placed on their lives, and praise God for the influence they have on you.

Incarnatio

INCARNATION ✝ LIVE THE WORD

Write a letter of encouragement to your pastor this week expressing your gratitude for the hard work he or she does. Encourage others from your church to do the same. Along with the letter, commit to pray each morning for your pastor.

PREACHING HIS NAME TO THE END

Listening for God through Acts 28:17–31

SUMMARY

P aul had come to the last stop on his journey—Rome. In his debates and trials before Jewish and Roman officials in Jerusalem, he appealed to speak to the highest ruler in the entire world at that time. He appealed to Caesar not because he had a charge to bring against the Jews (as he explained to the Jewish leaders in Rome) but because once again he followed the leading of the Holy Spirit and put himself in the place of certain suffering for the cause of Christ.

Even house arrest did not deter Paul from preaching and setting meetings with his enemies. Paul's consistent desire for people to hear and believe the word of Jesus Christ showed the motive and compassion that drove his ministry.

Luke's recording of Paul's ministry ended there in Rome, and only legend can fill in the blanks. We can only speculate on the manner of martyrdom, but one thing we know for certain: Paul preached the name of Jesus Christ until the end.

SILENCE ✝ LISTEN FOR GOD

As you quiet your heart today, keep your eyes open. Look around the room you are sitting in and remind yourself that God's presence fills every square foot of that room, every particle of air. He envelops you with His love, grace, and Spirit.

PREPARATION ✝ FOCUS YOUR THOUGHTS

Put yourself in the shoes of first-century Jewish leaders who were listening to Paul's arguments for Jesus as the Messiah. What reservations would you have to accepting Jesus as the Anointed One? What do you think your response to Paul would have been?

READING ✝ HEAR THE WORD

Rome was the world leader during the time of Paul's missionary journeys. Caesar was a god among the mortals of the nations. Paul was not just an ordinary Jew held captive under Roman rule. He was a Roman citizen, entitled to the protection and benefits given to other citizens. His appeal to Caesar, made during his questioning and trial under Festus in Caesarea, placed him on the biggest stage in the world before the largest known audience. Paul made the most of this great evangelistic opportunity.

Paul also continued his writing ministry, completing his letters to the Ephesians, Philippians, and Colossians, along with a personal letter to Philemon. These prison epistles shed light on Paul's experience as an "ambassador in chains" and tell stories of Paul preaching to his guards and to the Jews of Rome. Paul's work while imprisoned in Rome laid the foundation for many Christians who followed him in this capital city.

Read Acts 28:17–31. Take turns reading this passage aloud. Sense Paul's unstoppable passion for preaching the good news of Jesus Christ.

Meditation ✝ Engage the Word

Meditate on Acts 28:17–22

On finally making it to Rome, though shipwrecked and under guard, Paul wasted no time in meeting with the Jews to share with them the good news of Jesus Christ. Would you have contacted the group that opposed you and was responsible for your imprisonment? What underlying passion was driving Paul through his trials?

Read the sidebar quote from Mother Teresa of Calcutta. We often want peace, but we don't want to go through the process that brings it about. Living happily with friends is not true

> If you want to make peace, you don't talk to your friends. You talk to your enemies.
> —Mother Teresa of Calcutta

peace. What is true peace? Why was Paul continually making contact with the enemy?

Is there an enemy in your life with whom you need to make peace? What is holding you back from taking the first step in peace towards your enemy?

Meditate on Acts 28:23–28

What lessons can you draw regarding evangelism from Paul's meetings with these Jewish leaders in Rome? What was his approach? What is the connection between Jesus and the Law of Moses? Would the gospel of the New Covenant be easier to grasp if you had a greater understanding of the Old Testament?

Paul spoke of the kingdom of God. What is this Kingdom? What does it look like, and how are you a part of it today?

Read the sidebar quote from Horace Mann. Paul unswervingly followed the truth, even when it was rejected by his audience. The main source of truth for Paul was Scripture. What is your view of Scripture and truth? Does it matter what you think of the veracity of the Bible?

> Keep one thing forever in view—the truth; and if you do this, though it may seem to lead you away from the opinion of men, it will assuredly conduct you to the throne of God.
>
> —Horace Mann

Read the sidebar quote from Madam Anne Soymanov Swetchine. Scripture is riddled with paradox. The Jews listening to Paul's message were left holding two apparently contradictory truths: God is one and Jesus, whom they knew to be a man, is also God. No wonder they were divided. How can both statements be true at the same time? Do you struggle with allowing God to harmonize the paradoxes of the Bible?

> When two truths seem to directly oppose each other, we must not question either, but remember there is a third—God—who reserves to Himself the right to harmonize them.
>
> —Madam Anne Soymanov Swetchine

The idea of truth has been wrestled with by theologians and church leaders of late. What is your view of truth? Does your belief or disbelief in the concept of absolute truth affect your life? If yes, in what ways?

Meditate on Acts 28:29-31

The last words we have from Paul paint a beautiful picture of his ministry and passion for telling the story of Jesus. What would you want the last words written about your life to say? What do you have to do now to ensure the eulogy you desire?

> To die daily, after the manner of St. Paul, ensures the resurrection of a new man, who makes each day the epitome of life.
>
> —William Osler

Read the sidebar quote from William Osler. How did Paul die daily? Have you been making the most of every day? What in your life needs to change in order for you to live with the same passion and zeal as that of the Apostle Paul?

CONTEMPLATION ✝ REFLECT AND YIELD

Why did God's chosen people have such a hard time accepting His salvation through Jesus? Do you think we as the Church miss any messages from God because we are blinded by our own beliefs of who God is and how He should act? If yes, what do you think those messages are?

PRAYER ✝ RESPOND TO GOD

The community you live in is full of hearts hardened to the message of Christ's love and compassion. Hearts of members of your church family may also be hard. Pray for the hard-hearted, that God's Spirit would soften them and that they might be open to receive the grace of God.

INCARNATION ✝ LIVE THE WORD

Set up a meeting some time in the coming weeks with a Rabbi from a synagogue in your community. Discuss the person of Jesus of Nazareth, not in an argumentative manner, but with a humble spirit that seeks to understand the point of view of the Rabbi. You may want to meet with a messianic Jew first so you can better comprehend the background of the beliefs you will discuss with the Rabbi.

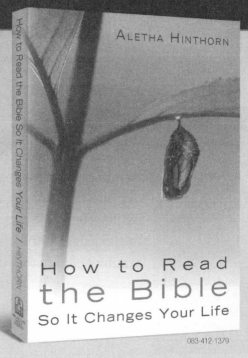

Acts

A Commentary for Bible Students

Philip A. Bence

An excellent resource for personal study, especially helpful for those involved in the teaching ministries of the church. Wesleyan Bible commentaries will encourage and promote life change in believers by applying God's authoritative truth in relevant and practical ways.

0-89827-195-9
Hardback

$15.99
252 pages

PHILIP A. BENCE is an ordained minister in The Wesleyan Church and a former missionary teacher at Kingsley College in Melbourne, Australia.

For additional volumes of The Wesleyan Bible Commentary series visit www.wesleyan.org/wph.

Order today from your local Christian bookstore!